Treasure Island

by Robert Louis Stevenson

CEFR level A2

Adapted by Karen Kovacs
for
Read Stories – Learn English

Read Stories – Learn English

Treasure Island: CEFR level A2 (ELT Graded Reader)
Original text by Robert Louis Stevenson
Adapted text © Karen Kovacs, 2024
Illustrations by Louis Rhead
Logo © Karen Kovacs, 2024

No part of this book may be reproduced, scanned or distributed in any printed or electronic form without permission. Please do not participate in or encourage piracy of copyrighted materials in violation of the author's rights. Thank you for respecting the hard work of the author.

CONTENTS

What are graded readers?   Page 4

Meet the author   Page 5

People in the story   Page 7

The story   Page 8

More stories   Page 78

Get a free story   Page 79

Words from the story   Page 80

WHAT ARE GRADED READERS?

Graded readers are books in easy English. They are written for learners of English and they have **vocabulary and grammar at your level**.

Each book has some new, more difficult words. There are **definitions** for these words at the back of the book.

WHY READ GRADED READERS?

- Studies show that learners who read in English **improve in all areas much more quickly** than learners who don't read.

- With graded readers, you **don't need a dictionary** so reading is more **relaxing**.

- The stories are all in **modern English**.

- You can learn vocabulary and grammar **in context** (this is the best way, according to teachers).

- Reading a book in English will improve your **comprehension**, your **fluency** and your **confidence**.

- The stories are **exciting** and reading them is **fun**!

Meet
the author

My name is Karen.

- I was born and brought up in England.
- I have a Master's degree in Linguistics.
- I have a teaching diploma and many years' teaching experience in the UK and abroad.
- I've written lots of books for learners of English.
- I speak Hungarian, French and Spanish so I understand what it's like to learn a foreign language!

ReadStories-LearnEnglish.com

More stories at the same level

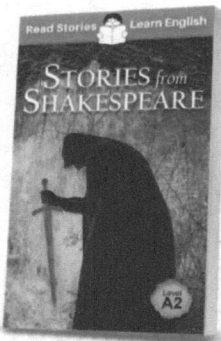

Shakespeare
in easy English

A modern
murder mystery series
in easy English

New words

When you see a word in **bold**, go to the back of the book. There you will find a definition of the word.

People in the story

Jim Hawkins
Billy Bones
Squire Trelawney
Doctor Livesey
Captain Smollett
Long John Silver
Ben Gunn

Treasure Island

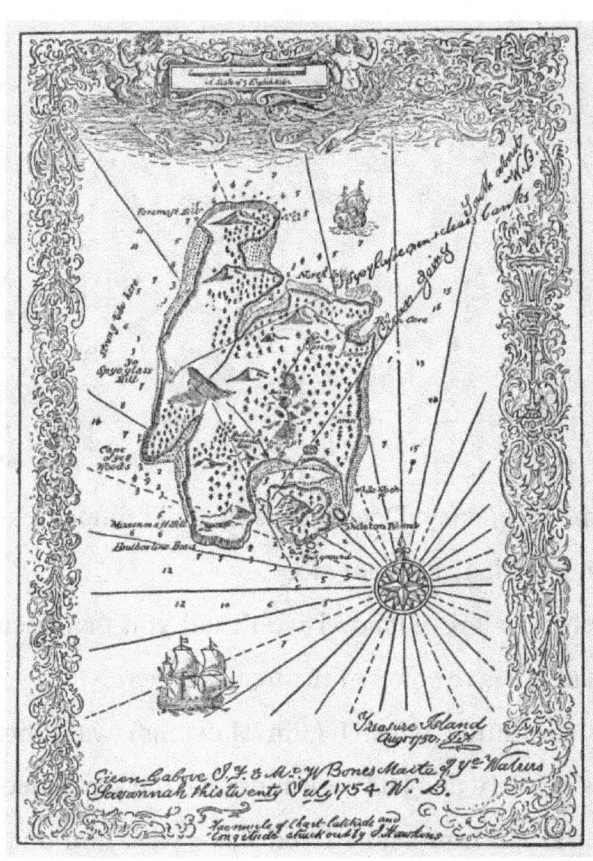

Chapter 1

THE "ADMIRAL BENBOW"

Squire Trelawney, Doctor Livesey and I found treasure on an island. This is our story.

Where is this island? I won't tell you that because we had to leave some of the treasure there.

It all started when I (Jim Hawkins) was thirteen years old. My dad had an **inn** next to the sea called the Admiral Benbow and I lived there with him and my mum. One day, an old **sailor** came to stay with us.

I remember him very clearly. He was tall and strong and he wore a dirty, old, blue coat. He walked **towards** the inn, looking carefully around him and singing a sailors' song:

"Fifteen men on the dead man's **chest**.

Yo-ho-ho and a bottle of **rum**!"

He came through the inn door, pulling his big, wooden sea-chest with both hands. "Give me a glass of rum," he said to my dad. My dad took him the drink and the man drank it slowly.

While he drank, he looked through the window. "What is he looking for?" I thought.

"Do you get many customers?" he asked.

"No, we don't," answered my dad, sadly.

But the old sailor was pleased about that. "Good!" he shouted happily. "Then I'll stay!"

My dad and I took the old sailor's sea-chest upstairs to one of the rooms. It was very heavy. Then we came back down, and the man said to us, "You don't need to know my name but you need some money." He threw three gold **coins** onto the table. "I don't want expensive food. Just cook me ham and eggs, and I'll drink rum."

He spent all his time outside, watching the sea. When he came back to the inn in the evenings, he always stood at the door and asked us, "Have you seen any sailors on the road today?"

The answer was usually "no" and he was pleased to hear it. If there was another sailor at the inn, he looked carefully through the door before he came in, his face worried. And he never talked to these other men.

In the evenings, he sat next to the fire and drank rum. Sometimes, he got **drunk** and sang sailors' songs really loudly. "Yo-ho-ho and a bottle of rum!" We all had to sing with him because, if we didn't, he got angry with us.

Before long, we **realised** that the man was a **pirate** and then we were more afraid of him than before. He often told stories of terrible things that happened at sea. "Pirates do horrible things to each other," I thought.

One day, he came to me and said, "Jim, listen. If you see a sailor with one leg, you must tell me immediately. I'll give you a silver coin every month if you do your job well. Don't tell anyone about this, do you understand?"

On stormy nights, when I heard the wind and the sea loudly through my bedroom window, I had horrible dreams about the man with one leg. I didn't know him but I was afraid of him. In my dreams, he ran after me and tried to kill me.

The pirate stayed for a long time and, after a few months, he stopped paying us. My dad didn't tell him to leave because he was afraid of him.

My dad was so worried about our guest that he became ill. Then, that year, the winter was long and very cold and this made my dad more ill than before. Every day, he was worse. The doctor tried to help him but he could do nothing. My dad died.

One cold January morning, the old pirate got up earlier than normal and went to the beach.

I watched him leave and then started tidying the room. **Suddenly**, the inn door opened and a man came in. He didn't look very strong and he only had three fingers on his left hand.

"Can I help you?" I asked.

"I want some rum," he answered. When I brought it to him, he said quietly, "Is my friend Billy Bones staying here?"

"I don't know your friend Billy Bones but there's a

man staying here."

"Does he have an old, blue coat?" he asked.

"Yes, he does," I said, beginning to feel worried. "But he's gone out."

"I'll wait for him," said the strange man. And he did. He waited behind the door, like a cat waiting for a mouse.

Finally, I saw our guest coming towards the inn. His friend took out a **sword** and held it in the air.

The old pirate came inside and the other man shouted, "Hey, Billy!"

Billy looked, surprised, and said, "Black Dog!"

"Yes, it's me!" answered the man.

"What do you want?" Billy asked, worried now.

"Sit down with me and let's talk," Black Dog said. Then he looked at me and said, "You need to leave now."

From the next room, I heard talking and then shouting. After a few minutes, I heard furniture breaking.

The next moment, I looked out the window and saw Black Dog running from the inn. Billy was running after him and they both had their swords in their hands.

Black Dog ran really fast and soon he was gone. Billy Bones stopped running and came back inside the house.

"He's gone, that ugly old pirate," he said to me angrily. "**I sailed** with Black Dog on **Captain** Flint's ship so I know he's a dangerous man. He'll be back later with his friends, the other men from Flint's ship. They want my old sea-chest."

Then he said, "Get me some rum."

I left the room to get his drink. A moment later, I heard a loud noise. "He's fallen down," I thought. I hurried back into the room and saw that I was right. Billy was on the floor, dead.

When I saw him, I started crying. It's strange because I didn't like the man. But I was still sad about my dad and I think I cried more for him than for Billy.

I went immediately and told my mum about Billy. She was very worried, of course. "The other pirates will come here and look for the sea-chest," she said.

"We should go and open it," I said. "He didn't pay us most of the time he stayed here. Maybe there's money in the chest. If there is, we can take some of it."

My mum agreed so we took the key from the dead pirate's coat and went upstairs to his room.

I opened the big, old chest and we looked carefully inside. We found lots of things, including clothes, an old Spanish watch and two **guns**.

"There's no money," my mum said sadly.

"Wait! Look!" I said. Under a coat, I found a bag of coins and a paper document.

My mum counted the money. There were coins from lots of different countries, such as silver ones from Spain called 'pieces of eight'.

"I won't take all the money," my mum said, starting to put some coins in her pocket. "We're **honest** people."

But before she could finish, we heard the sound of lots of heavy boots on the road. "The pirates are coming!" I told my mum.

We were really afraid. I picked up the document and we ran downstairs and out the back door. We **hid** behind a large tree and listened.

The men went into the inn and we heard them from outside. "Billy's dead!" one pirate said. Then they ran loudly upstairs and we heard the words, "There's the chest. Look inside!" And the next moment, a voice said, "It's not here!" One man started hitting the others and, in an angry voice, he shouted, "Look more carefully! If you find it, we'll be as rich as kings!"

I didn't know what 'it' was but they didn't find it. Soon afterwards, they left.

"What shall we do now?" my mum asked. "It's dangerous for us here."

"Let's go to Doctor Livesey's house," I answered.

When we arrived, our village doctor was having dinner with his friend, Squire Trelawney. The squire was very tall, very friendly and he talked a lot! He was also rich. "How can we help you?" he asked, smiling.

We explained everything.

"What were the pirates looking for?" asked the doctor.

"I don't know but perhaps it was this," I answered and I showed them the document from the sea-chest.

On the piece of paper, there was a map of an island, with instructions on finding it. On the map, there was a red cross and, next to it, were the words, "Flint's treasure here."

"I know that name!" said the squire. "Flint was a famous pirate, a very dangerous man. He stole lots of gold and silver from other ships."

The men were quiet for a minute, then the squire smiled and said, "We're going to Bristol tomorrow!"

"Why?" I asked.

"I'm going to buy a ship there," he explained, "then we'll sail it to the island and find the treasure!"

Chapter 2

I said goodbye to my mum and we left for Bristol, a large and busy city next to the sea.

While Squire Trelawney was looking for a ship, he told everyone in Bristol about our plans to find treasure.

When Doctor Livesey found out, he wasn't pleased. "Why do you always talk too much?" he said angrily to his friend. "We don't want people to know about the map or the island!"

"Stop worrying!" answered the squire in his loud voice.

The next day, he bought a ship called the *Hispaniola*.

"We planned to leave tomorrow but we don't have a **crew** to sail the ship for us," said the doctor.

"Yes, we do!" the squire told us happily. "The ship has **her** own crew, including a captain called Smollett.

But there weren't enough men."

"So what did you do?" asked the doctor.

"I was very lucky," he said. "I met an old sailor called Long John Silver. He's only got one leg, poor man, but he can work on the *Hispaniola* as a cook. And his friends are all sailors so they're coming with us too. They're ugly men but big and strong."

I was so excited about our journey that I didn't sleep much that night. I was going to sail across the ocean and look for **buried** treasure!

Early the next day, we all went down to the **harbour**. It was amazing to see so many beautiful big ships in the morning light.

Before I met Long John Silver, I was worried. "Billy Bones was afraid of a pirate with one leg. I hope it's not him," I thought. But when I first saw Long John, I stopped worrying immediately. This man was friendly and intelligent.

"I'm Jim Hawkins," I told him.

He smiled at me kindly and said, "Nice to meet you, Jim."

We all got onto the ship and there I met Captain

Smollett. He seemed angry with the squire but I didn't know why. However, I soon found out.

He came and spoke to the squire. "I don't like the crew that you chose," he said.

"Why not?" asked the squire, becoming angry too.

"I'm not sure that they are honest men."

"What's your reason for saying that?" asked the doctor quietly.

"I **have a bad feeling about** them, that's all," said the captain.

"A feeling?" shouted the squire. "I'm paying you to sail the ship. I'm not paying you for your feelings! Are you coming with us or not?"

"I'll only go if we can be safe," the captain explained. "I want to keep some guns and swords with us, in our part of the ship."

"He's worried about a **mutiny**," I thought.

"Yes, yes, alright," the squire answered and, a few hours later, we began our journey to Treasure Island.

While they worked, Long John's men all sang:

"Fifteen men on the dead man's chest.

Yo-ho-ho and a bottle of rum!"

The journey was long but the crew were all good sailors, the weather was pleasant and we had a strong wind.

Everyone liked Long John Silver. The doctor, the

squire, the captain, the whole crew, and me too – we all liked him.

He often talked to me on the journey. "You're a clever boy," he said to me one day. "I saw that when I met you."

I loved his pet **parrot**. The bird's name was Captain Flint and she liked to sit on Long John's **shoulder**. Her favourite phrase was "Pieces of eight! Pieces of eight!" She repeated it all the time.

"This parrot," Long John once told me, "has been to every country in the world and seen many terrible things."

The captain and the squire still didn't like each other and they didn't talk. But the captain **admitted** to me one day, "I was wrong about Long John's crew. They're actually good men and they work hard."

However, something happened one day that really **shocked** me.

We were nearly at the island and most of the crew were at the front of the ship, looking for it.

My work was finished and I was going to bed but I was a little hungry. There was a large **barrel** of apples on **deck**. It was nearly empty so I had to climb inside to get an apple. With the soft sound of the ocean and the ship moving slowly from one side to the other, I was soon sleeping.

Suddenly, there was a noise and I woke up. A man was now sitting with his shoulder against the barrel. Then I heard Long John's voice.

"Yes, that's right, I sailed with Captain Flint. Flint and his crew were all bad men. We did some terrible things … but we made a lot of money!" He was talking to a young crew member, not realising that I was listening from inside the barrel. "You're a clever boy. I saw that when I met you."

I was shocked – he was using exactly the same words that he used with me!

"I'm fifty years old now but I was like you once," he said. "And you can be like me. You can earn a lot of money if you work with me and my men. It's dangerous work but it's exciting!"

"Long John's a pirate," I thought, "and he's trying to **turn** that honest young sailor into a pirate!" I was afraid now. They might hear me inside the barrel. I tried to make no sound.

A third man joined the group. It was Israel Hands, one of Captain Smollett's men.

"The boy's going to work with us," Long John told Hands happily.

"That's great," he answered, "but tell me – when are we going to kill the captain and his men?"

"I'll decide that!" Long John answered angrily. "You're not very clever but you've got big ears so you can listen to me. We can't do it yet! I explained it all to you the other day. We can't sail this ship – only Captain Smollett can do that. And where is the map? We don't know, do we? The squire and doctor are hiding it. So how can we find the treasure when we get to the island?"

"Yes, that's true," said Hands.

"We'll arrive on the island," Long John said, "the squire and doctor will find the treasure, they'll bring it onto the ship and then ... we'll see."

"What will happen to the squire and doctor and the other men?" asked the young sailor.

"Well, we can leave them on the island and sail away without them," explained Long John, "or we can kill them."

"Billy Bones never left anyone on an island," said Hands. "He always killed his **enemies**!"

"I know," said Long John. "'A dead man can't hurt you,' he always said. And he was right. But now *he's* dead. So, you see ... we have to be careful."

"How many men are with us?" asked Hands.

Long John told him. Lots of crew members were

now pirates, exactly like Hands.

The three men were quiet for a moment and then Long John said to the young sailor, "Jump in the barrel and get me an apple, will you?"

My heart stopped! "Oh no!" I thought. "They're going to kill me when they find me."

However, at that moment, someone shouted, "I see the island!" I heard feet hurrying towards the front of the ship and I quickly climbed out of the barrel and joined them.

I saw two hills and, behind them, a higher one, half hidden in the night fog.

Long John came towards me and put his hand on my shoulder. "You're going to enjoy the island, Jim," he said, looking at me and smiling. "You'll be able to climb trees and swim in the sea."

I smiled politely but I knew now that he was a pirate.

I saw Captain Smollett, Squire Trelawney and Doctor Livesey on the other side of the deck so I went to talk to them.

"I have terrible news," I told them quietly.

"Let's go to my room," said the captain, looking worried.

A few minutes later, we were safely in his room. Nobody could hear us now so I told my friends about Long John's conversation and of course they were very shocked.

"Captain Smollett," admitted the squire, "you were right and I was wrong."

"I was wrong too," the captain said. "I had a bad feeling about those men but I didn't guess that they were pirates and wanted to start a mutiny."

The doctor turned to me and asked, "Are there any honest sailors left on the ship?"

"Yes, there are," I said and I told my friends the men's names.

"That's good," said the squire. "So that horrible man Long John Silver hasn't turned the whole crew into pirates."

"But there are only seven honest men and nineteen pirates!" said the doctor.

They all sat quietly for a while, their faces worried. Then the captain spoke. "We know Long John and his men are pirates but they mustn't find that out yet. If they do, they'll kill us."

We all agreed.

"The four of us and the honest crew members will have to **fight** the pirates," the captain said. "I don't know when but we have to prepare."

Chapter 3

When I woke up the next morning, I went up on deck and looked again at the island. Woods covered a large part of it and the beach was full of white **sand**. The sun was hot and birds flew in the air above me, looking for fish.

The captain told all the honest men about the pirates' plans for mutiny and he gave them a gun each. Some men stayed on the *Hispaniola*. The squire and the doctor wanted me to stay with them but I wanted an adventure. I hid in one of the small boats and **rowed** with the pirates and the rest of the honest men to the island.

I was afraid of Long John now so, when we arrived on the island, I ran as fast as I could into a wood.

"Jim! Jim!" Long John shouted behind me but I didn't answer him.

Away from the pirates, I began to enjoy myself and look around the island. I left the wood and found a sandy hill with only a few trees. No people lived on this island – there were only plants and animals, including dangerous snakes.

Suddenly, I heard voices and I hid under a big tree, as quiet as a mouse. One of the voices was Long John's and he was angry but I couldn't hear him clearly.

I moved nearer to them so I could see and hear them. Long John was talking to an honest crew member, Alan.

"Kill me like a dog, if you want," Alan said, "but I won't join you. I don't want to be a pirate."

He started walking away from Long John but he

didn't go far. The pirate **shot** him in the back, between his shoulders. He fell down, badly **injured** but not yet dead.

Long John hurried to him and **stabbed** him twice with his knife.

I was so shocked that I couldn't move for a while.

I realised that I had to leave. It was too dangerous

for me to stay there but where could I go? If I went to one of the small boats, the pirates might see me and shoot me. "I can't leave the island!" I thought.

I moved slowly and quietly away from Long John and then started running. After about one hundred metres, I saw a second dead body. It was another honest sailor. "Long John shot him too!" I thought, more afraid now.

I ran through another wood and suddenly, I saw someone – or something – hiding behind a tree. Was it a man or a monkey? I wasn't sure.

THE MAN OF THE ISLAND

The pirates were behind me and this strange person or thing was in front of me – I wasn't safe anywhere!

I stood and looked, and he (or it) watched me too.

Then I remembered that I had a gun and I took it out. The next moment, a man walked out to meet me. His skin was very brown from the sun and his eyes looked wild, like an animal's. His clothes were old and dirty. I moved back, afraid.

I was surprised but he didn't try to **attack** me. "Who are you?" I asked.

"Ben Gunn," he answered. "I haven't spoken to another person for three years!" He certainly looked very happy to see me.

"Three years!" I said. "What happened?"

"My crew members left me here on this island, alone," he said sadly. "I'm so bored of eating fruit and fish. I really miss cheese. I dream of it." He held my hand and asked, "Do you have any with you?"

"There's some cheese on our ship," I answered.

"Is that Flint's ship?" he asked, his face worried.

"It's not Flint's ship and Flint is dead," I said. "But some of Flint's crew members are with us."

"Not a man with one leg?" asked Ben.

"Yes, he's the cook. His name's Long John Silver." I explained everything to him.

"What's your name?" Ben asked me.

"Jim," I said.

He looked into my eyes and said, "Jim, I'm rich! And I can make you rich too! But we must be careful because, if Long John finds me, he'll kill me."

"How can this man be rich?" I thought. "I'm not sure that I believe him."

I didn't tell him but he saw my feelings in my face. "It's true, Jim," he said. "And if you take me home on your ship, I'll share the money with you."

"I suppose that's alright," I answered but I still wasn't sure.

"I was on Flint's ship when he buried the treasure," he said, his eyes big and wild. "He brought six strong men with him to the island in a small boat. They buried the treasure and then Flint shot them!"

I listened, shocked by his words.

"Billy Bones was one of the crew," he said, "and Long John too. We left together on the ship. Then, three years ago, I was on another ship and we saw the island. I told my crew members, 'There's treasure on that island,' and we came and looked for it. For twelve days, we looked but we couldn't find it. The men were all angry with me and they said, 'Ben, you can stay here and look for the treasure by yourself!' and they sailed away!"

"That's terrible," I said. "But I'm sorry – I can't help you because I can't get back on the ship. If I take one of the small boats, the pirates will see me and kill me."

"Ah, you can wait until it's dark and then use my boat!" Ben Gunn said with a smile.

"Your boat?"

"Yes. I made it myself and hid it," Ben told me.

The sun was going down and I felt cold. A moment later, we heard shooting. "They've started fighting," I shouted.

I didn't understand everything then. My friends only explained it to me later but I'll tell you now.

The captain, the squire and doctor were talking in the captain's room when Hunter, an honest sailor, came in. "Jim's not on the ship!" he said.

"What?" said the other men, shocked.

"He left on one of the small boats without telling us," Hunter explained.

"Oh no!" said the doctor.

"He's in danger," said the squire. "We have to go to the island and find him."

There were six pirates on the ship and they were sleeping in the afternoon sun. Careful not to wake them up, the squire, doctor and captain, and some other honest men, put some food, swords and guns in a small boat. They started rowing quickly towards the island.

Suddenly, the captain shouted, "Hands is on deck and he's going to shoot us!" And he was right – Hands was holding a gun and was ready to **shoot at** the men in the small boat.

Without waiting a second, the squire picked up a gun and shot at the ship. He didn't kill Hands but he killed another pirate.

Hands shot and hit the small boat. Water started coming in but this was not a problem because the boat was already near the beach. The men climbed out, with their guns and food above their heads, and hurried onto the sand.

The noise of the guns brought the other pirates to the beach. "Run!" shouted the doctor.

They ran through a small wood and, a moment later, the captain shouted, "Look!" In front of them, there was a wooden building. All around the building, there was a wooden **fence**.

"I suppose Flint's men built this years ago," said the captain. "This place will be very useful to us. We'll be able to shoot the pirates from inside but they won't be able to shoot us."

They ran towards the building, with the pirates' voices close behind them. A pirate shot one of our men, Tom, and two men carried him into the building. At the same time, the squire and the doctor tried to shoot the pirates. The squire hit one and the pirate fell down, dead.

The injured sailor lay on the floor of the wooden building, the doctor with him. "Am I dying, doctor?" he asked.

"I'm afraid you are," the good doctor answered sadly.

Then, without another word, Tom died.

The squire had a British **flag** with him and he put it on the roof of the building.

Soon, our enemies started shooting again, both from the island itself and from the ship. They could see the British flag on top of our building. They hit the fence and the building more than once but not my friends.

The next moment, they heard a voice. "Doctor! Squire! Captain! Is that you in that building?"

It was me! I climbed over the fence and joined my friends.

Chapter 4

My friends were pleased to see me again. I answered all their questions and I told them about Ben Gunn.

"Where is he now?" asked the doctor.

"I don't know," I answered. "He said goodbye and left."

"Well, if he comes back," the doctor said, "he can have this cheese." And the kind man put some cheese on the table for him.

Half the men sat next to the windows of the wooden building, their guns in their hands, waiting for the pirates. The rest of us went outside to bury poor Tom in the sand.

I was really tired so I slept well that night.

The sound of voices woke me up the next morning. "He's holding a white flag," someone shouted.

It was Long John with one of his men. They were

standing in the early-morning fog outside the building and the younger man was holding a white flag.

"I don't want to fight," the old pirate told us. "I just want to talk."

"Shall we believe him?" the squire said to us inside.

"Have your guns ready, men," the captain told us, "and I'll talk to him." He went outside to Long John and we followed. "What do you want?" he asked.

"I'm Captain Silver now," he answered.

"What?" said Captain Smollett. "No, you're not!"

"Yes, I am," said Long John. "You left your ship so my men decided that I am the captain of the *Hispaniola* now."

This made the Captain Smollett angry.

"Ah, Jim!" said Long John to me. "And the doctor. Hello! You're like a big happy family!" He laughed.

But Captain Smollett didn't laugh or smile. "What do you want?" he asked again.

"I want the treasure," Long John admitted. "And I want the map. If you give it to me, we'll share the treasure with you."

"No, you're not getting the map," our captain shouted angrily. "I've got a better idea. Bring all your men to this building. We'll keep you all here and, when we've found the treasure, we'll take you back to England. If you're lucky, you won't **be hanged**. That's the right thing to do and you know it!"

"I don't like your idea," answered Long John. "Instead, I think we'll leave on the ship and then you'll have to stay on this island!"

"You can't leave without us," the captain said. "You're not a real captain and you can't sail that ship. Now go away before I shoot you!"

Long John Silver wasn't happy but he left.

"Men," the captain told us, "I wanted to show Long John that we aren't afraid … but actually I am a little worried."

"Why?" I asked.

"Long John has more men than us," the captain explained. "There were lots of pirates at the start and we haven't killed many of them. Everybody, stand at the windows with your guns."

We stood at the windows for an hour. It was

uncomfortable and very hot.

Suddenly, a group of pirates ran out from the woods and started running towards the building. We shot at them and they shot back at us. We were lucky because they only hit the outside of the building.

However, a minute later, some pirates jumped over the fence and were soon inside the building. One of them attacked the doctor with a sword! But the doctor was a good fighter and the pirate fell to the floor with a big cut on his face.

"Get out!" the captain shouted to us. "Get out and fight them outside!"

I picked up a sword and ran out into the sunlight. A pirate cut my hand with his sword but I didn't stop fighting.

I ran to the back of the wooden building and, there, I **noticed** that there was a pirate in front of me, with his sword high above his head. "He's going to kill me!" I thought, but I didn't have time to be afraid.

I jumped to one side, then fell down the hill. When I got up, I looked up to the top of the hill and saw that we were winning the fight. One of our men was killing a big, strong pirate. Another shot a younger, smaller pirate. The doctor killed at least one pirate too.

The last pirate inside the building was running out, afraid. Then, there were no pirates left.

We ran back into the wooden building. The rest of the pirates might return so we couldn't leave it empty.

The captain was sitting on the floor, with the squire next to him. "He's injured," the squire told us sadly.

The pirates didn't come back so we were able to look after the injured men and make lunch.

The captain was badly injured but he wasn't dying. "He'll get better," said Doctor Livesey, "but he mustn't walk or move his arm for a few weeks."

After lunch, the squire and the doctor sat with the captain and had a long conversation. I couldn't hear them because I was on the other side of the room. Then the conversation ended, and the doctor picked up the map and his gun and left the building, walking into the wood.

I was really surprised. "Where is the doctor going?" I asked my friends.

They didn't answer me. Slowly, I began to feel that I wanted to leave the hot wooden building too.

I had an idea – I wanted to go and find Ben Gunn's boat. I put some biscuits in my pocket, picked up a gun and quietly left when nobody was watching.

I walked towards the east of the island. It was late in the afternoon, but it was still warm and sunny. I enjoyed my walk a lot.

Then I saw the *Hispaniola* in the harbour and I noticed that she had a pirate flag on her. This shocked me. "The ship belongs to the pirates now," I thought.

The sun started to go down. I knew that I had to hurry if I wanted to find Ben's boat that evening.

Finally, I found it, hidden by plants. It was round

and very small but also very light to carry.

At that moment, I had a new idea. "I'll take Ben's boat to the *Hispaniola* and **cut her adrift**," I thought, smiling to myself. "Then the pirates won't be able to sail away and leave us here."

I waited until it was dark, eating the biscuits from my pocket for dinner, and then carried the boat to the water.

While I did it, I heard Long John and some of the other pirates on the beach. They were sitting around a fire, and they were all singing sailors' songs and laughing. "Several of their friends died this morning," I thought, "but they're not sad." Captain Flint, the parrot, was on Long John's shoulder and making a horrible noise!

They didn't notice me while I rowed the little boat to the *Hispaniola*. I arrived next to the ship and heard pirates' voices from inside. "They're all drunk," I thought. I recognised one of the voices – it was Israel Hands. Suddenly, one of the men threw an empty rum bottle into the sea.

I listened more carefully and thought, "They're not

only drunk. They're angry as well." The pirates were shouting at each other.

I cut the *Hispaniola* adrift with my knife. It was quite easy to do. Soon, the big ship began to turn slowly and she moved towards my boat. This gave me an idea. Maybe I could climb up the side of the ship and look in one of the windows.

"It's strange that the pirates haven't noticed that their ship is adrift," I thought. However, when I looked inside, I immediately understood the reason. I saw Hands and another man. They were fighting and each man had his hands around the other man's neck.

The ship was moving through the sea more quickly now and I noticed that she was very close to the pirates on the beach. "I'm sure they'll see me," I thought. At that moment, I got back into the little boat, very afraid. I lay down in the bottom of the boat and waited to die.

I lay there for hours and finally I slept, dreaming of my home and the Admiral Benbow Inn.

Chapter 5

When I woke up, my little boat and I were at the south-west end of Treasure Island. It was hot again and I was really thirsty.

I looked up and saw the *Hispaniola* coming towards me. Somebody was sailing her around the island, back to the harbour. But then she turned around, the wind left the sails and she stopped in the water.

"The pirates are still drunk, I suppose," I thought, "so they can't sail the ship very well."

But where were the men? I couldn't see anyone on deck. They were probably sleeping. Maybe I could climb onto the ship and sail her back to her real captain, Captain Smollett.

I rowed to the ship and jumped onto the back part of her. I looked back and watched while the ship hit the little boat and broke it into pieces. I was on the *Hispaniola* and now I couldn't leave her!

Suddenly, I noticed two pirates. One of them was Hands. They were lying on the deck with rum bottles at their side. There was lots of blood on the wooden deck next to the men and I thought, "Are they sleeping or have they killed each other?"

A moment later, Hands woke up. "Ah, Mr Hands," I said, "good morning!"

He looked up at me angrily but said nothing. He was still ill from the rum and he was injured so he couldn't stand up.

"I am your new captain," I told him, "and I don't want this pirate flag on my ship."

I took it down while I spoke, then threw it into the sea.

Finally, Hands spoke. "That man's dead," he said, pointing to him. "I suppose, Captain Hawkins, that you want to get back to the island and I can help you sail the ship. You can't do it alone, can you?"

I admitted that I couldn't. "But I don't want to go back to the same harbour. I want to sail the ship to the smaller harbour in the north."

"Alright," answered the pirate. "Get me some rum

and some food and I'll help you."

I got myself some water too and then we began our journey.

We had a good wind and, soon, we were sailing the ship towards the north of the island without any problem. I was enjoying the pleasant weather and the beautiful views. And it was fun being captain of a big ship!

However, I had a bad feeling about Israel Hands. He was watching me carefully with his small, bright eyes and smiling strangely. What was he planning? He needed me to sail the ship but perhaps he wanted to kill me when we arrived in the harbour.

"Why did you stab that man?" I asked him, pointing to the pirate next to him.

"Well, a dead man can't hurt you, can he?" he answered, laughing.

The entrance to the harbour was not very wide so it was difficult to sail the ship into it. But, with Hands's instructions, I did it. We saw that this part of the island was full of trees.

"Sail the ship onto the sand, boy," said Hands.

And I did.

However, when I looked around, I saw the pirate behind me, holding a knife up in the air.

"I thought you couldn't stand up!" I shouted and he laughed, still moving towards me.

I took out my gun and shot at him but unfortunately I didn't hit him.

He was really near me now and I was afraid. Where could I go? I decided to climb the **mast**!

Hands was surprised by this and, of course, it was difficult for him to follow me. He did, however, but he could only climb really slowly.

Up the mast, I had time to get out my gun again. I held it up and said, "I'm going to shoot you in the head, Hands! A dead man can't hurt you, can he?"

I laughed and he stopped climbing.

But suddenly, he threw his knife at me. It hit my shoulder, went through my clothes and into the mast. I couldn't move.

I felt terrible pain but I shot my gun at Hands before it fell from my hands. The old pirate fell from the mast and into the sea, dead.

I looked down into the water and saw a fish or two swim past his body.

There was blood all over me and I felt sick. I pulled my shoulder from the mast and climbed down.

The ship was mine now and I didn't want the other dead pirate on the deck. It wasn't easy but I pulled him up and pushed him into the sea.

I looked down and saw Hands and his friend, next

to each other at the bottom of the sea.

The sun went down and it began to get cold. I climbed down from the ship into the sea. The water wasn't deep and I walked easily to the beach.

I was pleased – the ship was safe and there were no pirates on her anymore. I wanted to go back to the wooden building and tell my friends about my adventure. I wanted to hear them say, "What a clever boy! Well done!"

It was dark now but there was some light from the moon. I followed the river and soon found the building. It was strange, however, because, behind the building, I saw a big fire. I didn't understand and felt a little afraid. We never made big fires like that because we didn't have enough wood.

But when I looked inside the building, I felt better. I couldn't see much in the dark but I could see my friends lying on the floor, sleeping. With my arms in front of me, I walked in slowly. My foot hit something. It was someone's leg but he didn't wake up.

Then, suddenly, I heard a horrible sound. "Pieces of eight! Pieces of eight! Pieces of eight!"

Long John's parrot!

Long John woke up and shouted, "Who's there?"

I turned to run but I hit someone and he held me in his arms.

"Bring a lamp," said Long John, the parrot sitting on his shoulder. Finally, with the light from the lamp, I could see. There were six pirates in the room but my friends were gone. Were they all dead?

"Well, hello, Jim," said Long John Silver. "You've come to visit us. That's very friendly!" He laughed.

I didn't answer him. I stood with my back against the wall. I tried not to look afraid but I was.

"Listen, Jim," said Long John, "you're a good boy – clever, young and handsome, like I was years ago. So I'm happy to say that you'll have to stay with us. Do you know why? Because your friends are angry with you. You left them and they won't want you back now. They think that you've turned into a pirate!"

I was sad to hear this news but at least I knew that my friends weren't dead.

"Where are they?" I asked.

"I don't know," said Long John. "They left. And the

Hispaniola has gone too. She's not in the harbour."

I smiled at him. "You have the building, it's true, but you haven't been lucky, have you? You've lost your ship and lots of men, and you don't have the treasure. And how did all that happen, do you know? It was me!"

He looked at me, surprised. "What do you mean?"

"I was in the apple barrel and I heard you," I explained. "And I cut the *Hispaniola* adrift. And I killed the men on the ship. Kill me, if you want, but I'm not afraid anymore."

One of the pirates, Morgan, jumped up. "I'm going to kill you!" he shouted, holding up a knife.

"Stop!" shouted Long John. "Who's the captain here? Not you!"

"Morgan's right," said another pirate. "We should kill the boy."

Long John was really angry now. "Stop, I said!" Then he looked at each of them and said, "Fight me, if you want."

But nobody moved.

"What's wrong? Don't you understand English?" said Long John.

Again, they didn't answer.

"I like that boy," Long John said, pointing at me. "I like him and he's a better man than any of you. You're all rats! And if you try to hurt him, I'll kill you."

Nobody spoke for a while after this.

Then, the men started to talk quietly to each other. Long John and I were on the other side of the room so we couldn't hear them. Sometimes, a man turned to look at Long John, then turned back and started talking again.

"What are you all talking about?" asked Long John, after a few minutes, looking worried.

"We don't have to tell you that!" one of the men said.

Long John turned to me. "Those men are stupid but also dangerous," he said. "I'll **save** you from them. But I'll only do that if you save me from being hanged."

"I'll help you if I can," I told him.

"Good," he said, pleased. "Now, tell me: why did the doctor give me the map?"

He saw from my face that I was shocked.

"I know. It's strange, isn't it?" said Long John. "But it's true. He gave me the map."

Chapter 6

A little while later, the pirates walked towards us slowly, afraid of Long John.

"I won't eat you!" laughed Long John. "What's the problem? Tell me."

"We want a different captain," one of the men told him.

"Why is that?" asked Long John.

"Because the squire, doctor and Captain Smollett left and you didn't stop them!" the man explained. "And now, you want this boy to join our crew."

"Is that all?" asked Long John quietly.

"You're a bad captain," the man said, "but we want to be safe. We don't want to be hanged."

"There's a danger that you'll be hanged, it's true," answered Long John. "But if you think I'm a bad captain, you're wrong! Look at this!" and he took the map from his pocket and threw it onto the floor. I saw the red cross on it.

The pirates were shocked. Then they picked it up and started looking at it. They were so happy that they laughed like children.

"This is great," said a pirate called George Merry, looking at Long John, "but how can we take the treasure home? We've lost the ship."

"That's right," answered Long John angrily. "I got the map and you lost the ship. But you wanted a new captain so choose one now!"

"Long John!" they shouted. "Long John forever! We want Long John to be our captain!"

The old pirate smiled. "Alright," he said. "Now let's sleep."

I didn't sleep well because I was worried about the future. The next morning, a sound woke us all up. The doctor was at the door!

"Good morning, Doctor Livesey!" Long John said with a big smile on his face. "Come in, come in!"

The doctor walked into the building.

"Look, doctor," said Long John, "a surprise for you!

Jim is here!"

"Really?" the doctor said. "I'll talk to him in a minute, but first I'll see your men." And he checked all the injured men and gave them medicine.

Then he and I went outside to talk.

"What's wrong with Long John?" he asked me. "The man seems worried."

"He thinks that he'll be hanged back in England because he's done bad things," I explained. "But he has some good in him. He saved me from the other pirates last night."

The doctor looked me in the eye and asked, "Why did you leave us, Jim?"

"I'm sorry," I said, my head down. "I wanted an adventure."

"Don't worry," he said kindly, "but you mustn't stay here with those men. Jump over this fence and run away with me. Quickly!"

"No, I can't leave Long John Silver," I said. "He needs my help."

The doctor wasn't pleased.

Then I said, "The ship is in a harbour on the north

of the island. I moved her!"

"The ship?" said the doctor, surprised.

I explained everything to him and he listened carefully.

"Well done," he said, his hand on my shoulder.

"Stop talking now, you two," Long John said, walking towards us with Captain Flint the parrot on his shoulder. "That's enough."

And the doctor left.

Long John spoke to his men. "Let's go and get this treasure and then we'll try and find the ship."

They were all very excited but I was worried. "What will happen to me when they find the treasure?" I thought. "Maybe the other pirates will attack Long John Silver and me because they won't want to share the treasure with us. I'm a boy and he's only got one leg so we won't win against them."

Long John took four guns with him and a sword! The other pirates had guns and swords too but I had nothing. They were worried that I might run away. We walked slowly towards the place with the red cross on the map. It was far and it was a hot day, as usual.

After an hour, Long John stopped and said, "Which **direction** is the treasure? The map isn't very clear."

Suddenly, the man at the front of the group shouted loudly. "Argh!"

"Have you found the treasure?" Merry asked him, but the man sounded afraid, not excited.

When we arrived at his side, we saw, at the bottom of a tall tree, a human **skeleton**. Our hearts stopped for a moment.

"He's lying in a strange way," noticed Long John. And he was right. The skeleton's body was straight but its hand was pointing to the left. "Flint killed this man, then left his body here to show the direction of the treasure."

"This man was tall and he had blond hair," said Morgan. "It's Allardyce!"

"I think you're right," answered Long John quietly.

"Captain Flint was a horrible man," said Morgan. "Everyone was afraid of him. I remember, he always sang that sailors' song, 'Fifteen men'."

"I'm glad he's dead," said Long John Silver.

The men were a little worried after finding the skeleton but we started walking again, in the direction of its hand.

Suddenly, we heard someone singing. The voice came from the middle of the trees in front of us:

"Fifteen men on the dead man's chest.
Yo-ho-ho and a bottle of rum!"

The men's faces all went white. Two of the men held each other's hands.

"It's Flint!" said Merry, looking around him in every direction.

"He's dead so how can it be him?" shouted Long John. But he was afraid too, I could see.

The singing stopped.

"Come on!" said Long John. "Let's go and find that treasure. We'll be so rich! You won't ever have to work again in your lives!"

The pirates liked this idea and we started walking again.

I watched Long John's red, angry face and I thought, "He doesn't want to share the treasure with us. When we find it, he'll kill us all, take the treasure and sail away from the island."

We were very near the treasure now and some of the men started running. Then we heard them shout in surprise.

"What's wrong?" asked Long John.

But he didn't need to ask. When we looked, we saw that there was no treasure. There was just a big **hole**.

"Someone has taken it!" shouted the men. They were angry and they turned to look at Long John, their captain.

"We'll be rich, will we?" shouted Morgan. "How can we be rich? The treasure is gone!"

"You knew about this, didn't you?" Merry asked Long John.

It wasn't true but I could see that the other men agreed with Merry.

Long John started moving away from his men and

he took me with him. We now stood on one side of the hole and the five men were on the other side. Long John gave me one of his guns.

The next second, he shot Merry and he fell into the hole, dead.

Suddenly, the doctor and Ben Gunn joined me and Long John! "Come with us, quickly," the doctor told us. "Let's run to the boats."

We arrived at the boats and couldn't see the pirates anywhere. We sat on the sand while the doctor told us everything. "Ben Gunn found the treasure a long time ago," he said. "He carried it all to a **cave** and hid it there before we arrived on the *Hispaniola*."

"Ah, now I understand!" Long John said. "You gave me the map because it wasn't useful anymore."

"Exactly," the doctor admitted, smiling.

"And I sang the song from the trees," said Ben Gunn with a smile. "You thought I was Flint!"

We all laughed, then we got into one of the boats and rowed to Ben Gunn's cave. We went past the *Hispaniola* and I saw that she had a British flag on her again.

The squire was waiting for us. He spoke kindly to me and I was glad that he wasn't angry with me. But he was very angry with Long John. "You're our enemy," he shouted, "and I'd love you to be hanged. But we'll save you because you helped our Jim."

"Thank you," said the old pirate.

We all entered the cave. It was large and the floor was sandy. Captain Smollett was lying next to a fire, still badly injured. Then I saw that one side of the cave was full of coins and gold! This was Flint's treasure. "We came so far for this," I thought, "and seventeen men from the *Hispaniola* died to find it."

We had a delicious dinner that night and we all felt really happy.

The next morning, we got up early and started taking the treasure to the small boat. We rowed to the *Hispaniola*, put the treasure on the ship and then went back for more.

One man stood on a hill and watched. "If the pirates come," he said, "I'll shoot them." But they didn't come.

We worked for days. There was a lot of treasure! "We'll have to leave some of it here," said the captain. "We can't take it all – there isn't enough space."

One night, the doctor and I heard the three pirates,

singing, but we couldn't see them. "They're all drunk," said the doctor, "and I think they're ill as well."

"What's going to happen to them?" I asked.

"We have to leave them on the island," he answered. "We don't want another mutiny on the ship."

On the last day, we filled the ship with water and food from the island.

We started sailing away and then we saw the three pirates. They were watching us, their hands in the air. "Please, don't leave us!" they shouted. But, of course, we didn't go back for them.

Suddenly, one of them stood up angrily and shot at the ship. However, he didn't hit her because we were already quite far from the island.

I watched from the deck while the island became smaller and smaller. Soon I couldn't see it anymore and I felt pleased. We were safe now.

We sailed to Mexico and stopped there. We needed more crew. In the beautiful harbour, Mexicans came in little boats to sell us fruits and vegetables.

An hour later, we noticed that Long John was gone!

"He probably went to the beach in one of the Mexicans' boats," said the doctor.

"He won't come back," said the squire. "If he travels back to England with us, he'll be hanged."

"He's taken some of the treasure," Ben Gunn told us.

We were a little angry but actually we were happier without Long John on the ship. We never saw him again.

We found some crew in Mexico and sailed back to England without any more problems. We shared the treasure so every man got some.

Ben Gunn spent all his money in three weeks! We gave him some more and he bought his own inn.

Captain Smollett stopped working and soon got better. He lived a happy life, and the doctor and the squire did too.

I never want to go back to that terrible island. I'm too afraid. Sometimes, on a dark and stormy night, I have a bad dream and hear the voice of the parrot Captain Flint in my ears:

"Pieces of eight! Pieces of eight!"

THE END

More stories

A1 / Elementary

A2 / Pre-intermediate

B1 / Intermediate

B2 / Upper intermediate

VISIT MY WEBSITE

You will find:
- **information** about my **other books**
- a **free story**
- **free exercises** for this book
  (vocabulary exercises, comprehension exercises and notes about British culture)

ReadStories-LearnEnglish.com

Words from the story

admit (v)
agree that something is true, especially unwillingly

attack (v)
try to hurt using violence

barrel (n)
a large container, made of wood, with a flat top and bottom and curved sides

be hanged (phr)
be killed, as punishment for a serious crime, by having a rope around your neck and dropping down

bury (v)
put something into a hole in the ground and cover it

captain (n)
the person in charge of a ship

cave (n)
a large hole in the side of a hill, cliff or mountain

chest (n)
a large, strong box, usually made of wood; the upper front part of the body

coin (n)
a small, round piece of metal that is used as money

crew (n)
a group of people who work together to operate a ship

cut (a boat/ship) adrift (phr)
cut the ropes so that it is moving on the water but not controlled by anyone

deck (n)
the top outside floor of a ship (**on deck**, phr)

enemy (n)
a person of group that you fight against

direction (n)
the general position of a thing

drunk (adj)
having drunk so much alcohol that it is impossible to think or speak clearly

fence (n)
a wooden structure that divides two areas of land

fight (v)
be in a war or battle against an enemy; physically struggle with someone (**fight**, n)

flag (n)
a piece of cloth with a special design on it that is the symbol of a country or group

gun (n)
a weapon that is used for shooting bullets

harbour (n)
an area of water on the coast where ships can shelter (=stay safely)

have a bad feeling about (phr)
feel that something bad might happen but without clear proof

her (det)
(see *she*)

hide (v)
put something in a place where other people can't find it; go to a place where other people can't find you

hole (n)
a space in the ground, made by taking away the earth

honest (adj)
always telling the truth, and not stealing or cheating

injured (adj)
physically hurt

inn (n)
a pub usually in the countryside where people can stay for the night

mast (n)
a tall pole on a ship that supports the sails

mutiny (n)
when sailors do not obey their captain and take control of the ship

notice (v)
see or became aware of something or someone

parrot (n)
a tropical bird that can talk

pirate (n)
a person on a ship who attacks other ships at sea to steal from them

realise (v)
understand or become aware of a particular fact or situation

row (v)
move a boat through water using oars (=long pieces of wood with flat ends)

rum (n)
a strong alcoholic drink made from the juice of sugar cane

sail (v)
travel on a ship using sails (=using the wind) (**sailor**, n – a person who works on a ship; **sail**, n – a sheet of material that catches the wind and makes a ship move)

sand (n)
very, very small pieces of rock on a beach that are soft and usually white or yellow, found on a beach (**sandy**, adj)

save (v)
keep someone safe from harm or death

she (pro)
Ships are usually referred to as *she/her*, especially by sailors. It's an old tradition and they do this because they see the ship as their mother, protecting them at sea.

shock (v)
surprise or upset someone

shoot (v)
fire a gun (**shoot at**, phr v – fire a gun in the direction of someone or something but maybe not hit them/it)

shoulder (n)
the part of your body between the top of your arm and your neck

skeleton (n)
all the bones in a person's body

stab (v)
push a knife into someone's body

suddenly (adv)
quickly and unexpectedly

sword (n)
a weapon with a long metal blade (=cutting part) and a handle

towards (prep)
in the direction of somebody/something

treasure (n)
a collection of valuable things such as gold and silver

turn into (phr v)
become something different

www.ingramcontent.com/pod-product-compliance
Lightning Source LLC
Chambersburg PA
CBHW011959090526
44590CB00023B/3783